BONKERS

BOFFINS,

INVENTORS

and other Eccentric Eggheads

WAYLAND

Published in paperback in 2016 by Wayland
Copyright © Hodder and Stoughton Limited 2016

Wayland, an imprint of Hachette Children's Group
Part of Hodder & Stoughton
Carmelite House
50 Victoria Embankment
London EC4Y 0DZ

Commissioned by: Debbie Foy
Design: Rocket Design (East Anglia) Ltd
Illustration: Alex Paterson
Proofreader/indexer: Susie Brooks

A catalogue for this title is available
from the British Library
509.2'2

10 9 8 7 6 5 4 3 2 1

ISBN: 978 0 7502 8391 5

Printed in England

MIX
Paper from
responsible sources
FSC
www.fsc.org FSC® C104740

An Hachette UK company
www.hachette.co.uk
www.hachettechildrens.co.uk

All illustrations by Shutterstock and Dover Publications, except:
10, 12, 36, 39, 47, 49, 53, 61, 73 and 88.

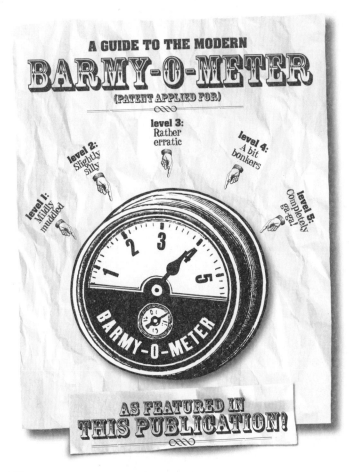

A GUIDE TO THE MODERN
BARMY-O-METER
(PATENT APPLIED FOR)

level 1: Mildly muddled

level 2: Slightly silly

level 3: Rather erratic

level 4: A bit bonkers

level 5: Completely ga-ga

BARMY-O-METER

AS FEATURED IN THIS PUBLICATION!

How do our Boffins, Inventors and other Eccentric Eggheads rate on the Barmy-O-Meter?

Read on to find out!

BONKERS BOFFINS THROUGH THE AGES

There have probably always been bonkers boffins – or at least, boffins who SEEMED bonkers at the time. The caveman who first suggested adding sharpened points to spears probably got a few odd looks from his friends. The person who first suggested that invisible messages could be sent through the air (which today we call 'radio') definitely did. A government minister wrote, 'to the madhouse' on his proposal.

In this book you'll meet some of the foremost kooky scientists and imaginative inventors. Of course, when we say they were bonkers, we don't mean they were *actually* mad. Our collection is made mostly of three kinds of eccentric egghead:

1. The ones who really were very, um, eccentric

Want to meet the scientist who fell in love with a pigeon (and felt sure she loved him back)? How about the world-famous inventor whose last breath was preserved forever inside a test tube?

They're both in here, and lots more like them.

2. The ones who came up with crazy ideas

If you've ever considered that the world is in desperate need of a device for keeping your moustache dry while you drink tea, think again – someone else has already come up with the idea. Or how about testing the strength of electricity by touching it with your tongue? (Don't try this at home!)

These ideas may SOUND loony – but they actually happened.

3. Boffins with bonkers life stories

Some of our eggheads weren't bonkers themselves, but had such a rollercoaster ride through life that their stories are utterly amazing. If you'd like to know more about the scientist everyone thought had been kidnapped by the Russian Secret Service, but who had actually left town to escape his debts, he's here. So is the very poor girl from Poland who went on to win TWO Nobel Prizes, plus lots of others.

As well as all this, you can find out about some crazy inventions that didn't catch on. An organ powered by tiny explosions, perhaps? Or can we interest you in a steam-powered lawnmower? Or how about a purse with a pistol hidden inside?

Intrigued? Turn the pages to find out more.

Bonkers Boffins...

...in their own words!

'Watson. Come over here. I need you.'

No, it's not Sherlock Holmes calling his faithful assistant, Dr Watson. These were the first words transmitted by Alexander Graham Bell's spanking new telephone. Bell was speaking to his assistant in the next room, to test the first-ever working telephone.

BONKERS BOFFINS

(who don't really exist)

Victor Frankenstein

Victor Frankenstein was a wealthy Swiss scientist who was utterly fascinated by the power of electricity to move the human body. But Victor didn't simply want to make dead bodies move ... he wanted to bring one to life!

Victor began to assemble the parts for the V. Frankenstein Build-A-Body kit™. An arm here, a leg there, a head from somewhere else – stitched them all together and, hey presto, a body! (Admittedly, an odd one, 8 feet tall and looking as if it had been built of spare parts – because it had.) All that was left was to bring it to life using a massive jolt of electricity from a lightning strike.

The trouble was, when the body came to life, Victor was so scared he ran away. The body, which now it was alive had turned out to be a monster, wandered off to do terribly monstrous things – for example, killing people. After Victor Frankenstein himself finally died, the monster floated off on an iceberg.

When all's said and done, it's probably a good job Victor Frankenstein is just a character in the novel *Frankenstein* by Mary Shelley, from 1818.

The scientist with a loose screw

Archimedes of Greece (287–212 BC)

Imagine this: you're out and about doing your shopping one morning. Suddenly, a dripping-wet philosopher runs past, waving his arms in the air. To make matters worse, he's wearing only a beard. Would you be shocked?

Not if you were doing your shopping in the ancient Greek city of Syracuse, you wouldn't. You'd probably just think, 'Huh. There goes that bonkers philosopher, Archimedes. He must have had another good idea.'

In fact, Archimedes had just discovered that if you put something in a full container of water, exactly its own volume of water spills out. He had found this out by sitting in a full bath. Archimedes was so excited by his new idea that he leapt straight out and ran into the streets to tell everyone.*

Archimedes, don't go using all the hot water!

✳ Some people say that there's no proof this REALLY happened – but they're just spoiling a good story.

8

Archimedes didn't only come up with good ideas. He also invented all kinds of useful things. These included:

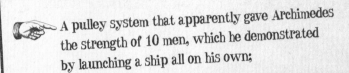 A pulley system that apparently gave Archimedes the strength of 10 men, which he demonstrated by launching a ship all on his own;

A kind of ancient Greek super-yacht, with pleasure gardens, a gym, and even a temple on board;

The Archimedes Screw, a tube with a spiral screw inside it. When the spiral was turned, it lifted water up the tube. The Screw was good for pumping water out of the (slightly leaky) super-yacht, and for irrigating crops.

In 214BC, the Roman army laid siege to Syracuse. Archimedes got to work inventing weapons that would make them go away. But poor Archimedes met a suitably bonkers end. The Romans finally invaded Syracuse in 212BC, and their commander sent a soldier to get for Archimedes. But he refused to come – whereupon the solider got so annoyed, he stabbed Archimedes to death...

INVENTIONS THE WORLD TURNED OUT NOT TO NEED

THE MOUSTACHE-GUARD TEACUP

Back in Victorian times, men liked nothing more than to grow a great, big, fat, bushy moustache.

While these moustaches looked VERY handsome, they did come with a problem attached – a problem that became clear as soon as a gentleman decided he'd like a bowl of soup for lunch. By the end of the meal, his moustache had collected all kinds of debris, and looked like one of those nets you might use for dredging dead leaves out of swimming pools.

Various solutions were tried: metal moustache protectors, special spoons, and even teacups with a moustache-guard built in. But the only real solution was ... a razor.

BARMY RATING: 3 OUT OF 5

BARMY-O-METER

Moustache guard

11

Alexander Graham Bell, Scotland (1847–1922)

In the 1870s, the Scottish inventor Bell came up with a way of using electricity to transmit speech, and wanted to register his invention before anyone else. He finally got it to the Patent Office (where new inventions were registered) on 14 February 1876. HOWEVER, on the very same day, Elisha Gray filed a patent for *his* version of the telephone.

Me first!

No, it's me!

Patent Office

Bell managed to persuade people that his patent had been delivered first, and that the telephone was his invention. Within a few years, the Bell Telephone Company had spread across the USA.

Was Alexander Graham Bell a bit dastardly?*

It has been suggested that Bell wasn't quite the kindly inventor that people thought. In particular, he's been accused of dodgy dealings over his invention.

☞ It is said that an Italian-American inventor, Antonio Meucci, invented the telephone long before Bell, but didn't patent it to protect his invention. It's also said that Bell once shared a workshop with Meucci, and might have 'borrowed' some of his ideas.

☞ It has also been suggested that Bell's patent was registered ahead of Gray's because the man making the decision at the Patent Office was heavily in debt to Bell's lawyer, and that this might have affected his thinking...

☞ *The truth is probably that ideas rarely develop in a complete vacuum. They are sparked by other inventions and changes in technology. So it's not unusual for more than one person to have a similar idea at the same time.

The tale of the high-flying pen

These new biros are top notch, old boy.

László Biró, Hungary (1899–1985)

Back in the 1920s, journalists couldn't record people's voices to remind them what interviewees had said. They had to write everything down – REALLY quickly! László Biró, a Hungarian journalist, got sick of the way his pen made this difficult by constantly spurting ink, which took ages to dry.

Biró came up with a design for a pen with a ball at the tip, instead of a nib. The ball rolled and picked up ink as he wrote. Genius! But at first no one wanted to buy these new 'biros'.

Then the Second World War came along.

For Biró, there were good things and bad things about the war. He was forced to move to Argentina, to get away from the Nazis who had invaded Hungary. But on the plus side, people started buying his pens! The British realised that they worked much better than fountain pens at high altitude, and ordered loads for their bomber crews to use.

In 1945, Biró sold the patent to his design to a Frenchman called Bich. Bich started a pen company called ... Bic.

DR GUILLOTINE AND HIS HUMANE BEHEADING DEVICE

During the French Revolution (1789–99), one of the things the Revolutionaries were terribly keen on was beheading enemies of the Revolution. (At first they beheaded mainly aristocrats, but they soon ran out of those and started beheading each other instead.)

The Revolutionaries used the guillotine, named after the man who first suggested it, Dr Joseph-Ignace Guillotine. Everyone thinks he actually invented it – but he didn't. Similar devices had been used in England, Italy, and Scotland for centuries.

The man who invented reading by pinprick

Louis Braille, France (1809–52)

Louis Braille wasn't bonkers but what he invented was bonkersly brilliant as it transformed the world for millions of blind people.

Ever since he could walk, Louis Braille had been fascinated by his father's workshop. He was always wandering in there, picking up tools and trying to make things. Then, one day when he was just 3 years old, there was a terrible accident.

Louis was trying to make a hole in a thick piece of leather using a sharp, pointed awl. To make sure he was doing it properly, he bent close to the leather. As he pressed down, the awl skidded off, and stuck into his eye.

The local doctor bound up Louis's injury, and sent him to see a specialist in Paris. But the wound got infected and it spread to Louis's other eye. Within a few weeks, Louis was blind. In the 1800s this was a terrible thing: blind people found life very difficult, since it was almost impossible for them to find work.

Louis, though, was a clever boy. He was invited to be a student at one of the first-ever schools for blind children, in Paris. There he learned how to read, by tracing the raised outlines of letters on paper. This system was better than nothing, but Louis became determined to improve it.

So, he invented a code in which every letter could be represented by a maximum of six dots, in two columns of three dots each, side by side. At first the dots were made by pricking holes in paper, using an awl similar to the one that had blinded Louis. But later, a typewriter-like machine would be used.

Louis's system of reading and writing for the blind became known as Braille. It revolutionised life for blind people, and is still used around the world today.

An early Braille machine

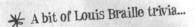

※ A bit of Louis Braille trivia...

Louis was a brilliant musician, and could play the cello and organ. In fact, he was the official organist at two Paris churches.

CrackPot
Quiz Question

Q. When Samuel Born arrived in the USA from Russia in 1910, what made him famous ...?

a) He came up with a new way to make chocolate sprinkles – revolutionising cupcake design around the world;

b) He came up with a way to coat ice cream in chocolate – revolutionising pudding around the world;

c) He invented the 'Born Sucker Machine.'

It's all three! The fabulously named Born Sucker Machine was a device for automatically putting the sticks into lollipops. Bizarrely, even though he lived on the East Coast of the USA, Born was given the Freedom Of The City Of San Francisco (on the West Coast) in recognition of this achievement!

18

Roxey and the royal underwear

Breathe in, ladies!

Roxey-Ann Caplin, Canada (1793–1888)

How many people can say they went from the wild prairies of Canada to making underwear for the Queen of England?

Back in Victorian times, women inventors didn't have a lot of room to operate. Men mostly kept the test tubes, electrical engines, and things that might explode to themselves. But one area where women WERE allowed to experiment was with underwear design.

Roxey-Ann Caplin was born in Canada, but later moved to London, England. She became a corset-maker. Corsets were much in demand in those days, by people who wanted to find a way of holding their tummies in. Lots of wealthy people were rather portly, as a result of only exercising by walking to the dinner table, then eating too much when they got there.

Ms Caplin kept coming up with improvements in corset design. Her shop in London's Berners Street became popular with London's most important people. And that's how Roxey-Ann came to make corsets for the Queen!

The man who gave the world peanut butter

George Washington Carver, USA (1864–1943)

The first thing to say is, we all owe George Washington Carver a big, big vote of thanks for inventing peanut butter. But of course, he did EXCELLENT other stuff, too.

George had an amazing life story. He was born into slavery, some time during the American Civil War. When the Civil War ended, slavery was abolished, but life was still very hard for black people. Nonetheless, in 1891 George got into Iowa State University – the first black person ever to attend.

George spent his time discovering crops that local farmers could grow instead of cotton, such as soybeans, peanuts and sweet potatoes. He also came up with things the new crops could be used for, including hundreds of recipes and uses for the peanut alone. Peanut shampoo, perhaps? Or a drink of peanut milk? OK, no, maybe not…

By 1921, George had become so well known that he was giving US Congressmen advice about agriculture. He was catapulted to international stardom, and became quite a celebrity.

He met Presidents Theodore Roosevelt, Coolidge, and Franklin Roosevelt.

The Crown Prince of Sweden came to the USA and studied under George.

George became friends with the millionaire carmaker Henry Ford.

When George died in 1943, the USA was busy fighting the Second World War. Even so, it was decided that there should be a National Monument to him. It was the first for a black person, and the first for anyone other than a former President. The monument is in Diamond, Missouri.

The high-society inventor

Josephine Cochrane, USA (1839–1913)

Josephine Cochrane was a society dame, who threw a lot of dinner parties. The servants were ALWAYS chipping her plates and bowls while washing up. If only someone would invent an automatic dishwashing machine to replace the clumsy servants!

When her husband died, Josephine desperately needed cash (she'd spent all the money on dinner parties). She and a workman she'd hired went into the shed in her back garden and – like an 1800s version of *Wallace and Gromit* – emerged some time later with a dish-washing machine. And unlike some of Wallace's inventions, it worked.

In fact, Josephine's machine worked SO well that big restaurants and hotels started ordering them. Before she knew it, Josephine had to start up her own company, just to keep up with all the people who wanted her dishwasher.

INVENTIONS
THE WORLD TURNED OUT NOT TO NEED

SATNAV WITHOUT SATELLITES

In the 1920s, cars were starting to become popular among ordinary people. But road signs hadn't caught up yet, and it could be tricky to find your way around. The answer? An early – very early – version of satnav.

Of course, it couldn't actually use satellites: those hadn't been invented yet. Instead, the motorist wore a watch-like device, which held a teeny map of his or her route. The map was long and thin, and wound around two little rods, like a tiny medieval scroll. Drivers unrolled the map as they drove, revealing the next bit of their route.

It's not clear why the navigational watch didn't catch on. Maybe road signs improved, or people started using proper maps... Or maybe it was just TOO DANGEROUS trying to unwind a teeny scroll while driving.

THOMAS CRAPPER AND HIS FLUSHING TOILET

Thomas Crapper (1836–1910) was a London plumber. His firm, Crapper & Co, had the world's first ever bath, toilet and sink showroom on London's Kings Road. Most people think that Crapper invented the flushing toilet – but they're wrong.

Sir John Harington (see page 51) invented the first flushing toilet in 1596, and the first practical one was designed in the 1770s.

People are also wrong to think that Crapper gave his name to a rude word for poo. In 1846, when Crapper was only 10 years old, toilets were already being called 'crapping' houses.

The scientist who brought people back to life

Giovanni Aldini, Italy (1762–1834)

These days, if people want an evening out they might go to the cinema, or maybe a concert. Back in the 1800s, though, nightlife was a bit more varied. How about going to see a dead body being brought back to life, at Giovanni Aldini's Corpse Reanimation Show?

Giovanni Aldini was an Italian scientist fascinated by electricity. In particular, he was interested in 'galvanism', the use of electricity to move muscles. Aldini's most famous demonstration of galvanism happened in 1803, when he got hold of the body of a murderer.

The murderer's body was laid out, and Aldini started to 'reanimate' it. First he applied electric current to the face – and the corpse's mouth moved. He even appeared to blink! Next the murderer's right hand made a fist, which he raised into the air. Then – with the help of more electricity – the dead body's legs were made to twitch, almost as if he was trying to run away.

How's that for a night out you'd never forget?

The woman who discovered radioactivity

Marie Curie, Poland (1867–1934)

Marie Curie is one of the top boffins ever. She won TWO Nobel Prizes. She discovered all about X-rays. She was the first-ever woman professor at the Sorbonne, one of the world's top universities. Look at these brilliantly bonkers facts about her:

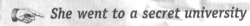

She went to a secret university

Marie was born in Warsaw, Poland. At the time, Poland was part of Russia, which insisted that students learn Russian subjects, and wouldn't let in women. So Marie instead went to the 'Floating University' – a top-secret study group that was constantly changing its location, taught Polish subjects and allowed women.

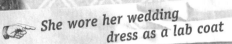

She wore her wedding dress as a lab coat

In 1891, having spent years studying and saving, Marie left for Paris, France, to study at the famous Sorbonne University. There, she met Professor Pierre Curie. They fell in love and got married. Marie used the blue dress she'd got married in as a lab coat for years afterward.

👉 *She discovered radioactivity in a leaky shed*

By this time, Marie was doing groundbreaking scientific work. She tried to discover all she could about X-rays and radioactivity. She and Pierre worked in an old shed with a leaky roof, but nonetheless discovered new radioactive elements. Since these seemed likely to be able to cure cancer, this was generally seen as A Good Thing and made her famous:

👉 In 1903, Marie won the Nobel Prize for Science – the first woman ever to do so.

👉 In 1906, after Pierre was knocked down by a carriage and killed, Marie took over his job as professor at the Sorbonne.

👉 In 1911, Marie's work in chemistry won her a second Nobel Prize. She was the first person ever to win two.

👉 *Her notebooks are STILL bonkersly dangerous*

Marie was one of the first people to work with radioactive materials. In those days, no one understood how deadly these were. But today, Marie's old notes are STILL so dangerously radioactive that you have to wear protective clothing to look at them. Even her old cookbook is kept safe in a lead-lined box that shields people from its radioactivity.

Perhaps it's not surprising that when Marie died in 1934, it was because of her long exposure to radioactive material.

Charles Darwin, England (1809–82)

Most people like tortoises: they're cute, in a slow-moving, defenceless kind of way. Charles Darwin liked them too. In fact, he liked them so much he used to eat them. But we're getting ahead of ourselves...

As a scientist, young Charles didn't have a very promising start. In fact, one of his teachers wrote that, 'This boy is dull' – meaning a bit stupid. Hmm.

Things didn't get much better when young Charles went off to university to train as a doctor. He wasn't really all that keen on doctoring – what he liked to study were rocks and animals. So one of the professors arranged a place for him on a ship called the *Beagle*, which was just about to set off on a voyage of exploration around the world.

When the *Beagle* reached the Galapagos Islands, Charles noticed that the animals seemed to be specially adapted to the foods that were found there. Second, there were giant tortoises everywhere. At first, Charles contented himself with riding around on them – but he soon discovered that tortoises were good to eat, too.

tortoise, anyone?

By the time the *Beagle* got home, Charles had come up with the germ of a Big Theory: the Theory of Evolution. He thought that animals evolved because they had to compete for food. Only the fittest species and animals got enough food to survive, and these then passed on their superior characteristics to their young. Over thousands of years this led to, for example, the beaks of birds changing shape.

Back in England, when Charles published his Big Idea it caused uproar. The Bible, which most people believed, said that God had designed animals. Charles was saying that something else had done it. In the end, though, he has turned out to be right, and the Church of England eventually apologised for the misunderstanding.

What's for lunch?

Mind you, they took their time. By then, he'd been dead for 126 years.

Help!

The Gourmet Club

STRANGE DARWIN DINNERS

At university, Darwin was a member of the Gourmet Club (also sometimes known as the Glutton Club). They met once a week to eat things you couldn't get at a normal restaurant, such as hawk and owl. Darwin carried on his strange eating habits while on his travels, and scoffed down some very rare animals…

From the Darwin menu

BROWN OWL

This was said to have been so revolting that it led to the Gourmet Club being disbanded!

PUMA

Say 'giant cat' and it sounds quite a lot less appetising…

ARMADILLO

Darwin said that the lightly roasted armadillo he ate in South America 'tasted like duck'.

LESSER RHEA

Darwin had been trying to find the rare Lesser Rhea for weeks. Supplies ran low, so he killed what he thought was a Greater Rhea to have for dinner. Halfway through eating it, Darwin realised it was actually a Lesser Rhea. Oops! He sent the remains home to London, like a half-eaten takeaway.

CrackPot
Quiz Question

Q. What first made people sit up and notice the Pullman railway sleeping carriage in the 1800s ...?

a) Its inventor had been inspired by his own name: he was called George Pullman, and he had invented something that pulled men along;

b) It was the first kind of train carriage to feature in a disaster movie;

c) It was used to transport the body of an assassinated US president.

---

c) In April 1865, President Abraham Lincoln was assassinated in a theatre. A Pullman carriage was used to transport his body from Washington, D.C. to Springfield, Illinois. Answer a) is also true, but isn't what made the carriage famous. As for b), movies hadn't been invented when the Pullman appeared in 1867.

Last breath caught

Thomas Edison, USA (1847–1931)

When Thomas Edison died, the carmaker Henry Ford persuaded Edison's son Charles to capture his last breath in a test tube. You can still see the test tube in the Ford Museum today – though it's not known whether the last breath has leaked out by now. How would you check?

As a boy, Thomas Edison worked selling sweets and newspapers on trains. He wanted to be an inventor so much that he even built a secret laboratory in one of the empty wagons. When it caught fire, the conductor threw him off and Edison lost his job.

Next, Edison became a telegraph operator (after being taught how to use one by a man whose son Edison had saved from being run down by a train). He worked at night, which left him plenty of time for inventing. Unfortunately, another experiment went wrong, and Edison ended up spilling acid on his boss's desk. The next morning: **'Edison, YOU'RE FIRED!'**

This is a phonograph (see opposite page for details).

... in a test tube

Not all of Edison's experiments went wrong: he soon began coming up with electrical devices that **DIDN'T** burn things down. Edison worked almost non-stop, and only slept for a few hours each night. His inventions included:

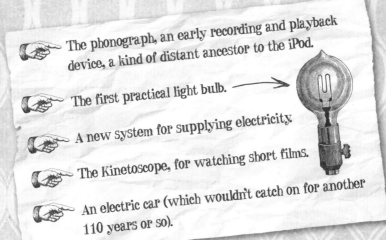

The phonograph, an early recording and playback device, a kind of distant ancestor to the iPod.

The first practical light bulb. ⟶

A new system for supplying electricity.

The Kinetoscope, for watching short films.

An electric car (which wouldn't catch on for another 110 years or so).

Edison was even once said to have invented a machine that could turn soil into food, and water into wine. Newspapers across America printed news of this amazing device – before discovering it was a spoof!

Bonkers Boffins...

...in their own words!

'I have not failed. I have just found 10,000 ways that won't work.'

Thomas Edison reminds everyone that even when an invention doesn't work, you learn something.

(Edison was famous for working so hard at trying to find solutions to problems that he sometimes fell asleep standing up!)

The strange case of Albert's brain

Albert Einstein left strict instructions that when he died, he was to be cremated and his ashes scattered.

What actually happened when Albert died in 1955 was that Dr Thomas Harvey at Princeton Hospital removed Einstein's brain. Without permission! Harvey then persuaded Albert's son that this had been a good idea.

Unfortunately, Princeton Hospital ALSO wanted Albert's brain. When Harvey refused to hand it over, they sacked him. Dr Harvey and the brain then began a trek around the country that lasted for the next 40 years. Along the way, bits and pieces got shaved off and used for research.

Finally, in 1998, the brain was returned to Princeton.

 A little more Albert trivia:
Einstein is said never to have worn socks.

The bonkers boffin who pretended he wasn't...

Albert Einstein, Germany (1879–1955)

Try to imagine what a bonkers boffin looks like. Perhaps old with crazy white hair and a distracted expression? That could be Albert Einstein you're imagining.

Einstein is the most famous scientist who ever lived. He improved, expanded on, and explained the work of Galileo, Newton and Curie, plus a bunch of other major-league boffins.

He was born and raised in Germany, but disliked it so much that he dropped out of school, moved abroad and told the government he no longer wanted to be a German citizen. He then failed his exams to college, which isn't a very good start for a genius scientist.

See! We told you he doesn't wear socks.

Later, Einstein did get a job as a professor in Germany, where he spoke out against the new Nazi government's treatment of Jews. In return, it seems likely that they planned to assassinate him, and may even have tried.

Since he wasn't keen on being assassinated or sent to a concentration camp, Einstein moved to the USA. He became a US citizen in 1940, and lived there for the rest of his life, working on science and campaigning for peace.

Einstein is most famous for his General Theory of Relativity, which is so difficult to understand that it can give you a nosebleed. Einstein himself once said that: *'If you can't explain it simply, you don't understand it well enough.'* But it might be best to take this with a pinch of salt, since his explanation of Relativity was: *'When you are courting a nice girl, an hour seems like a second. When you sit on a red-hot cinder, a second seems like an hour. That's relativity.'* Hmm.

Albert became so famous that people approached him in the street to ask for an explanation of 'that theory'. He got so sick of it that he eventually started replying: *'Pardon me, sorry! Always I am being mistaken for Professor Einstein!'*

BARMY-O-METER

BARMY RATING: 2 OUT OF 5

Michael Faraday, England (1791–1867)

When Michael Faraday left school at 13 he got a job in a bookshop and read STACKS of science books – especially about the fascinating subject of electricity. While other boys his age were climbing trees and getting into scrapes, Michael was hanging out at the Royal Institute, where famous scientists gave lectures. The star inventor of the day was Humphrey Davy. After learning of Michael's interest in science, Davy offered him a job. It involved doing experiments and Michael loved it.

When Davy died in 1829, Michael continued with his passion for electricity and magnetism. There were no tools for measuring electricity, so Michael touched electric objects with his hands, tongue and even his eyes to find out what would happen. He also chased electrical storms around London, in an attempt to understand how they worked.

Michael Faraday proved that there was only really one kind of electricity (most people thought there were several). He was also the first scientist to realise that electricity and magnetism were some kind of invisible force field. Sadly, by the 1860s Michael was suffering from an illness that affected his mind. He found it increasingly hard to think clearly or to remember things. His health deteriorated quickly and he died in 1867.

... to chase storms!

INVENTIONS
THE WORLD TURNED OUT
NOT TO NEED

THE PISTOL PURSE

Back in the late 1700s, highwaymen were a menace on lonely roads. Travellers dreaded hearing their famous warning cry, 'Stand and deliver! Your money, or your life!' Unless, that is, the traveller was carrying a pistol purse.

From the outside, this purse looked like, well, a purse. But cunningly hidden inside it was a teeny little pistol. You could take it out as though about to hand over your valuables – then let the highwayman have it in a way he DIDN'T expect!

The only problem was that the pistol was really, really tiny, so it was tricky to shoot accurately. And it only held one shot, so you didn't get a second chance. If you missed, or the highwayman had brought a friend, you'd be in BIG trouble!

'I believe I can fly'

Abbas Ibn Firnas, Spain (810–887 AD)

You'd have to be a bit bonkers to cover yourself with feathers, put on a pair of wings, and have a go at flying – but that's what Abbas Ibn Firnas did. What's more, he glided 'a considerable distance'. Unfortunately he hurt his back on landing, and the flying experiment was cancelled indefinitely.

And as if flying wasn't enough, Firnas also became a doctor, a poet, and a musician, and he:

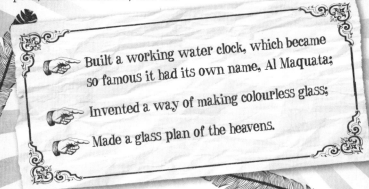

Built a working water clock, which became so famous it had its own name, Al Maquata;

Invented a way of making colourless glass;

Made a glass plan of the heavens.

To cap it all, he apparently made miniature clouds, thunder and lightning using machines in his basement. Bonkers!

How sloppy science saved the world

Alexander Fleming, Scotland (1881–1955)

I can't find a THING in this place!

Like a lot of scientists, Alexander Fleming wasn't ALL that tidy. In fact, his lab was a monumental mess. Which is a good job – because if it hadn't been, he might not have changed the course of medicine!

One day, Alexander got back from a month's holiday to discover that a strange thing had happened. He'd left a load of lab dishes piled up in a corner instead of clearing them up properly, and mould had grown on one of them. The dish had contained bacteria – which, for some reason, the mould seemed to have killed off.

At first, Alexander called the active ingredient in the mould 'mould juice'. Later, he gave it a proper scientific name: penicillin. It was the first-ever antibiotic. Today, antibiotics are used to cure gangrene, tuberculosis, syphilis, typhoid, pneumonia, and thousands of other deadly illnesses.

Bonkers Boffins...

...in their own words!

'When I woke up just after dawn on September 28, 1928, I certainly didn't plan to revolutionize all medicine by discovering the world's first antibiotic, or bacteria killer. But I suppose that's exactly what I did.'

Alexander Fleming describes his almost-accidental discovery of penicillin in 1928.

A life of wee and blood

Galen, modern-day Turkey (c.130–210 AD)

Only the most famous people can get away with just the one name. Rihanna, Jay-Z (OK, that's one-and-a-half), Madonna and … Galen?

Well, he was famous back in Roman times. Galen was a doctor, who learnt his trade stitching together wounded gladiators. He came up with some surprising medical discoveries. Surprising for ancient Rome, anyway:

 Urine is formed in the kidneys.

 Arteries carry blood, rather than 'the breath of life' as some people thought at the time.

 The larynx is the source of people's voices (this did become obvious when it was later renamed the 'voice box').

Galen later became a kind of doctor to the stars, personal physician to the BIGGEST celebrities of the Roman world – the Emperors. Three of them, in fact: Marcus Aurelius, Commodus and Septimius Severus.

Mad about rubber

Charles Goodyear, USA (1800–60)

Charles Goodyear was determined to find a way of making rubber useful. At the time it was soft and sticky, and came apart too easily. So Goodyear mixed rubber gum with magnesia. That didn't work very well, so what did he do? He sold all his furniture, moved his family into a guesthouse, and went to live alone in New York.

Determined to succeed in New York, Goodyear added magnesia then boiled the rubber in quicklime and water. That didn't work either. So then he dipped the rubber into nitric acid, to form a protective outer layer. This almost worked – but not quite.

Eventually, in 1844, Charles Goodyear was hard at work trying to come up with the ideal rubber compound and he *accidentally* spilled a mixture of rubber, sulphur and lead onto a hot stove. Bingo! It made JUST the right kind of rubber. He carried on trying – rarely successfully – to make a fortune from rubber for the rest of his life.

☞ GOODYEAR TRIVIA...

The Goodyear tyre company, founded almost 40 years after his death, was named in honour of Charles Goodyear in 1898 – but he had nothing else to do with it!

BONKERS BOFFINS

 (who don't really exist)

Dr Henry Jekyll

What if you could separate out the bad bits of your personality? What was left behind would be a purely good, kind, generous person – the sort who would play with their kid sister when she was bored, or hand in homework on time. That's what Dr Henry Jekyll hoped to achieve with his special potion.

Sadly, things didn't work out quite like that. The potion turned Dr Jekyll into Mr Hyde: a person who had no good in him at all, who was always throwing his weight around, beating people up or murdering them. Then Mr Hyde would turn back into the same old Dr Jekyll again.

Even worse, the transformation started to happen WITHOUT the potion. You'd be having a walk with nice Dr Jekyll, when suddenly he'd turn into Mr Hyde and

46

kill you. Very inconvenient. The only way to put a stop to it was for Dr Jekyll/Mr Hyde to kill himself.

What a good job he's just a character in the book *Strange Case of Dr Jekyll and Mr Hyde* by Robert Louis Stevenson, from 1886.

'Look out below!'

Galileo Galilei, Italy (1564–1642)

The scientist and inventor Galileo Galilei was born in the town of Pisa, Italy. He was interested in the speed at which things fall. To check his ideas, he climbed the Leaning Tower of Pisa with stones or cannonballs of different sizes, then dropped them to the ground.

The big and small balls hit the ground at the same time! It may not sound that exciting, but it was big news back then. This was because it went against the ideas of the Catholic Church's approved philosopher, Aristotle. And in Italy, in the 1600s, it REALLY wasn't a good idea to disagree with the Church.

Aristotle and the Church also said that the Earth was at the centre of the Universe. Then Galileo started saying that the Earth actually went round the Sun. Uh-oh. Galileo knew he had to be careful, so he put forward his theories in a book called *Discourse*, which took the form of a debate between three people. In the book only one of the three said the Earth went round the Sun.

Discourse hadn't gone down well with the head of the Church, the Pope. Looking back, it was probably a bad idea to give the character in *Discourse* who put forward the Pope's point of view the name Simplicio. In English, you can translate *Simplicio* as The Simple One, or The Fool. Gulp.

48

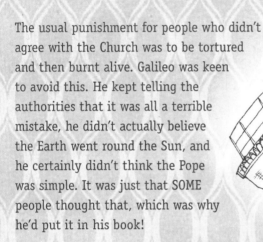

The usual punishment for people who didn't agree with the Church was to be tortured and then burnt alive. Galileo was keen to avoid this. He kept telling the authorities that it was all a terrible mistake, he didn't actually believe the Earth went round the Sun, and he certainly didn't think the Pope was simple. It was just that SOME people thought that, which was why he'd put it in his book!

In the end, Galileo was placed under house arrest for the rest of his life, and had to read seven sections of the Bible once a week for the next three years.

 Just time for one more Galileo fact...

You can still see the middle finger of Galileo's right hand in the Museo Galileo in Florence, Italy. If you want to, that is.

Crackpot Quiz Question

Q. Stubbins Ffirth (1784–1820) is an American doctor famous for ...?

a) His terrible spelling;

b) Drinking vomit;

c) Being the first person to perform a face-lift operation.

The answer is b). Yeuw. He was trying to show that the deadly disease yellow fever wasn't infectious. To prove it, he smeared cuts on his body with vomit, urine, blood, and saliva from yellow-fever sufferers. Then he thought drinking the vomit, and not catching yellow fever, would REALLY show people he was correct.

All it ACTUALLY showed was that Ffirth was bonkers: yellow fever is infectious, but only when injected into the bloodstream, for example by mosquitoes.

Elizabeth I's 'saucy godson'

Sir John Harington, England (1561–1612)

Queen Elizabeth called John her 'saucy godson', because he was always writing rude plays and poems. In fact, one of John's poems was **SO** rude that he was sent away to think very hard about what he'd done.

Instead, John actually spent his time dreaming up a new invention. It was a toilet – that flushed! It was the first known flushing toilet, so of course English people were highly suspicious. Very few were made, and it was much more popular in France.

Next, John went to Ireland, to fight Irish chieftains and their allies, but the fighting ended in a truce. When the commanders got back to London, the Queen gave them the hairdryer treatment.

By this time John had got into a lot of debt. He decided it would be easier to leg it than pay the money. It all worked out OK, though. Queen Elizabeth died, and the new king, James I, gave John lands that meant he could pay off his debts.

Maybe his nickname should really have been 'Lucky John'?

INVENTIONS
THE WORLD TURNED OUT
NOT TO NEED

THE REPEATING CANNON

You know what it's like. You're in the middle of an important battle, on the brink of victory, but then your artillery falls silent. What's going on? They've only all stopped to reload at the same time – DISASTER!

Unless, that is, you happen to be in possession of a new repeating cannon. It's mounted with four barrels, pointing forward, left, right, and behind. As the forward-pointing one is firing, the other three are reloaded. Then the barrels spin around ready for another barrel to point forward and fire.

What could POSSIBLY go wrong with an idea like that?

53

BONKERS BOFFINS

(who don't really exist)

Willy Wonka

What kind of loony inventor would have a nut room in his chocolate factory, where squirrels throw Bad Nuts (and anything else that comes into their hands but isn't a nut) down a rubbish chute? Willy Wonka, that's who.

Willy's other inventions include:

- Everlasting Gobstoppers
- Lollipop Bushes
- Jellybean Plants
- Lickable Wallpaper
- Cows that produce Chocolate Milk

No wonder his factory is sealed off from the outside world, for fear of spies stealing the great ideas! And what a shame these great inventions only existed in the mind of Roald Dahl, who wrote *Charlie and the Chocolate Factory* in 1965.

WONKA TRIVIA:

The idea of a secretive chocolate factory owner was based on reality. In the 1920s, rival British chocolate makers Cadbury and Rowntree often sent spies (pretending to be employees) into each other's factories, to try and steal their secrets.

A heroic engine

Hero of Alexandria, Egypt (c. 10–70 AD)

We don't know much about Hero of Alexandria. No one is even 100% sure when he was born. What we do know about are some of the amazing things he invented. Hero is most famous for his aeolipile. This was a very early – perhaps the first ever – steam-powered, rocket-style engine. It worked by heating water in a chamber with two curved nozzles sticking out of the sides. As the water boiled, the steam jetted out of the nozzles, causing the chamber to spin around.

Hero's aeolipile appeared over 1,600 years before the steam-powered engines of the Industrial Revolution. But although the ancient Egyptians knew all about child labour, they hadn't discovered other key elements of the Industrial Revolution. Without things like factory ownership and stovepipe hats, it was impossible to have an Industrial Revolution of their own.

Hero came up with all kinds of other things we'd recognise today:

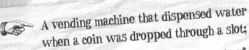

A vending machine that dispensed water when a coin was dropped through a slot;

A syringe for measuring out amounts of liquid or gas;

A powerful pump that could be used for squirting water at fires.

Now you know what an aeolipile looks like!

The architect, city planner and great thinker...

Robert Hooke, England (1635–1703)

As a child, Hooke caught smallpox – a deadly disease that left him deformed. Then his father died when Hooke was just 13. He decided to go to London to seek his fortune...

Hooke turned out to be extremely clever, and got into Westminster School. He was brilliant at maths and art, and skilled with his hands. One story says that Hooke once took apart a clock, made a wooden model of each part, and assembled them. The clock told the time.

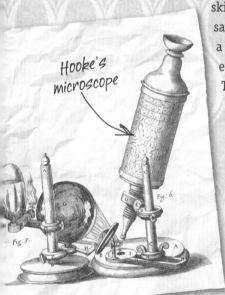

Hooke's microscope

Later, Hooke built a powerful microscope. His beautiful, accurate drawings of things he'd seen were published in a book called *Micrographica*. It was a smash hit – the first-ever science bestseller. His microscopic investigations led him to discover and name 'cells' in plants. He also began to understand how fossils were formed.

In 1666, much of London burnt down in the Great Fire. But the King asked Hooke and his old university friend Christopher Wren to come up with a plan for rebuilding the city. Wren got most of the glory, partly because of Hooke's reputation for being extremely grumpy and a bit stinky. (It was easy to be stinky in London in the 1600s: very few people washed more than once every few weeks.)

Sadly, the next thing Hooke did was to get into a dispute with Sir Isaac Newton (see page 74–75). Sir Isaac didn't like competition – so when Hooke claimed that Newton had got some of his ideas about gravity from Hooke, it didn't go down very well. The two fell out, and when Hooke died, all the portraits and writings of his at the Royal Society mysteriously disappeared.

The President of the Royal Society was none other than, Sir Isaac Newton.

Well, hello there

The nutty doctor

John Harvey Kellogg, USA (1852–1943)

Dr John H Kellogg and his brother invented cornflakes, back in the 1890s. However, John had far more than cereal on his mind ... He wanted people to be healthier and so he opened a health spa. Today, some of his ideas have people running a mile – to get away, not to get fit!

Just a couple of Kellogg's health fixes:

Be careful what you put in your body. Avoid anything tasty, as tasty food will only get you overexcited. Nuts ARE allowed. Nuts will one day save the human race from starvation.

Keep yourself clean, outside and – yeuw – inside. Have regular enemas (i.e. have liquid squirted up your bottom to clean it out). Start with a water enema. Follow this with a yoghurt enema, which will replace all the good bacteria you've just flushed out using water. (Which may make you wonder why it was a good idea to flush them out in the first place...)

By the time Kellogg died in 1943, his health spa was – perhaps unsurprisingly – struggling to find people willing to sign up to these ideas.

INVENTIONS
THE WORLD TURNED OUT
NOT TO NEED

THE SPHERICAL VELOCIPEDE

In the 1800s, the first bicycles were known as velocipedes. They didn't work all that well as pedals hadn't been invented yet, let alone tyres or gears. Still, fashionable gentlemen really enjoyed whizzing around on their pedal-less two-wheelers, like toddlers on balance bikes.

Why, then, we ask, did someone think the Spherical Velocipede was a good idea? It was a see-through sphere with a rod inside it for the rider to sit on. The rider moved the device by walking forward – which makes you wonder – why not just walk?

BARMY RATING: 4 OUT OF 5

An egg clock for a queen

Ivan Kulibin, Russia (1735–1818)

Ivan was a clever lad, despite not having been to school. He started life as an inventor by making toys in his attic, when he was a kid. Then he got interested in clocks.

One day, Ivan thought he'd make a clock shaped like an egg. Most people might give this to their mum, or maybe their best friend. Ivan decided to give HIS special clock to Catherine the Great, Ruler Of All Russia. As it was Ivan's first egg-shaped clock, this was a bit of a gamble. If she liked it, Ivan would be made. If she didn't, he'd be stuck in Nizhny Novgorod, where he lived, forever.

Fortunately, Catherine liked the clock. In fact, she liked it so much that she demanded Ivan move to the capital city, St Petersburg, and take charge of her Academy of Sciences.

Cool clock Ivan!

Catherine the Great, Ruler Of All Russia

A list of some of Ivan's inventions:

☞ A single-arch bridge over the River Neva, with a span of 298 metres. A model was built, and it worked brilliantly. Catherine was so pleased with it that she had it put in the Tauride Gardens, where she liked to go walking. Sadly, the actual bridge never got built: Ivan had forgotten that the technology for such a giant structure didn't yet exist. Oops!

☞ A cart powered by a man pushing on pedals. (Actually, to be strictly accurate, it was powered by a servant pushing on pedals – rich people didn't like to do that sort of thing.) The cart shared many features with the first cars, though those wouldn't appear for another 100 years or so.

☞ An artificial leg, for a friend of Ivan's who'd lost his leg while he was away at the Russo-Turkish War.

In 1801 Ivan gave up his job and headed back to Nizhny. He was planning to build a Perpetual Motion machine, one that would never stop working. This is impossible, but sadly Ivan spent all his money and died before he found that out.

The boffin who

Gottfried Leibniz, Germany (1646–1716)

Back in the 1600s, if you were clever but poor (like Gottfried), the best thing to do was get the support of someone very rich. This usually meant some sort of aristocrat. Fortunately, aristocrats liked to have one or two extremely clever people around – they thought it made them seem clever by association.

What Gottfried was really very good at was mathematics. He came up with a new branch of maths called calculus. He published details of it in Europe's top magazines for boffins. Everyone was very impressed – except Sir Isaac Newton (see page 75), who was VERY annoyed. Sir Isaac said that he'd actually invented calculus in 1671, but hadn't bothered to tell anyone. Plus, oh yes, he called it 'fluxions'.

The argument turned into a complete hissy fit. London's Royal Society decided to investigate, since Newton and Leibniz were both members. The Society's report said that Newton was definitely the person who'd

I call it 'calculus', you call it 'fluxions'.

invented calculus

invented calcul … er, fluxi … whatever you call them! The report was written by a leading member of the Royal Society. His name?

Well, since you ask, it was… Sir Isaac Newton.

The argument about calculus wouldn't have mattered all that much if it wasn't that Gottfried's boss happened to be heir to the throne of England. To make matters worse, in 1714 George Louis actually BECAME King of England.

This was what's known as a Sticky Situation:

 Sir Isaac, as England's (and the world's) top boffin, was part of George's entourage.

 As Court Counsellor, so was Baron Gottfried (who'd picked up a title of his own along the way).

Nothing spoils a state banquet like two top mathematicians throwing their food at each other, so they had to be kept apart.

In the end, George solved the problem by telling Gottfried he couldn't come to England just yet. Not until at least a BIT of the family history George had asked him to write all those years ago was finished.

When Gottfried died a couple of years later, he still hadn't managed it.

INVENTIONS
THE WORLD TURNED OUT
NOT TO NEED

THE PYROPHONE

You'll probably guess why this unusual musical instrument from the 1800s didn't really take off when you hear its nickname – 'the explosion organ'.

The pyrophone worked in a similar way to an ordinary organ, but instead of being powered by pumped air, it was powered by small explosions. ('Just small ones, nothing to worry about...' the maker probably said.)

Most pyrophones ran on propane gas, but some used hydrogen or gasoline. It must have been quite a nerve-wracking experience sitting down to play one for the very first time.

CrackPot Quiz Question

Q. Johann Conrad Dippel (1673–1734) is famous as a bonkers boffin because ...

a) He was born at Frankenstein Castle, and spent his life trying to discover ways to bring dead bodies back to life – making him the inspiration for the book *Frankenstein*?

b) While trying to discover the secret of immortality, he actually discovered a new kind of blue dye instead?

c) He claimed that souls could be transferred from one body to another using a special funnel?

It's all of the above. Dippel had a busy life; he was also imprisoned by the Catholic Church for heresy (a breeze compared to the usual sentence, which was being burnt at the stake); accused of being a grave robber and having a pact with the Devil; and described by an old friend as a 'vile devil' ... who attempted wicked things! No wonder some people think that when Dippel died, it was because he'd been poisoned.

That magnificent man and his flying machine

Otto Lilienthal, Germany (1848—96)

Imagine you're living on the far outskirts of Berlin in the 1880s. It's Saturday, and you're bored. You can't loaf about in a shopping mall as they haven't been invented yet – but you could go and watch that mad inventor Otto Lilienthal trying to fly!

Otto had been fascinated with flight for years. When they were boys, he and his brother had built feathered wings and tried to take off. Otto studied the way birds fly, and in particular how they glide. Then he started building gliders on the same principles. At first they didn't work that well – but Otto was still able to glide about 25 metres. Within a couple of years, he was going 10 times as far.

Sadly, it all ended badly. After three successful flights on a warm August day, Otto lost control of his glider, fell to the ground and died of his injuries three days later.

Look, I did it!

Bonkers Boffins...

...in their own words!

'No one can realize how substantial the air is, until he feels its supporting power beneath him. It inspires confidence at once.'

Otto Lilienthal, not long before finding out that the air WASN'T that substantial after all.

The inventor who helped

Guglielmo Marconi, Italy (1874–1937)

Back in the late 1800s, the idea that communications could pass invisibly through thin air seemed absolutely bonkers. When Guglielmo Marconi told a government minister it was possible, the minister wrote, 'To the madhouse' on the proposal, and threw it away.

Guglielmo's investigations began by building a secret laboratory in the attic of his parents' country house. He must be one of the few boffins to have been helped in his work by the family butler, but that's exactly what happened.*

After a great deal of experimenting, Guglielmo and the butler managed to set up a system that could transmit Morse code signals across the attic via radio waves. Guglielmo was so excited, he woke his mother in the middle of the night to give her a demonstration.

Hey, Mum, wake up!

Zzzz ... that's lovely, son.

✳ When Marconi later won a Nobel Prize for his work, the butler didn't get a share.

Titanic survivors

Guglielmo was sure his work could be used to send communications. This would make life much easier for everyone. But when he sent his idea to the Italian government, no one replied. So Guglielmo did what any self-respecting boffin would do. He went off to England in a huff.

In England there was a lot more help available than in Italy. Within a year of his arrival, Guglielmo had managed to send a signal 16 kilometres across the Bristol Channel. By 1902, he had sent a signal across the Atlantic. And in 1912, Guglielmo's invention played a crucial part in rescuing survivors from the *Titanic* when it sank.

The *Titanic* had two Marconi wireless operators on board. As the ship went down, they began to send distress signals. These were picked up by another ship with a telegraph operator on board, the *Carpathia*. The *Carpathia* picked up many survivors. Britain's Postmaster General said that:

'Those who have been saved, have been saved through one man, Mr Marconi, and his marvellous invention.'

An early Morse code machine

71

The inventors who were full of hot air

Joseph-Michel & Jacques-Étienne Montgolfier, France (1740–1810 & 1745–99)

Most people might watch their sheets drying over a fire and think little of it. Not Joseph Montgolfier. HE thought: 'I believe I can fly.' And you know what? He was right.

His interest had been sparked by the way the heat from the fire lifted the sheets. What if you could get hot air into a big bag? Would the bag float upward in the same way as the sheets?

In 1783, a Montgolfier balloon carrying Jacques-Etienne took off for the first time. But the balloon was tied to the ground – the Montgolfier brothers weren't bonkers enough to fly their own balloons. For that they had to find a total daredevil. And that's when Pilâtre de Rozier turned up...

Pilâtre de Rozier (1754–85) was a minor French nobleman. No one would ever have heard of him if he hadn't set TWO amazing world firsts – one good, the other, well ... not so good:

Amazing world first no.1

On 21 November 1783, de Rozier and another nobleman, the Marquis d'Arlandes, took off in a Montgolfier balloon. They flew about 9 kilometres, and reached a height of 900 metres or more. It was the first-ever free flight made by humans. De Rozier was well and truly bitten by the flying bug.

72

On another balloon flight he and a companion went higher (3000 metres), further (52 kilometres), and faster (70 kilometres/hour) than ever before.

Amazing world first no.2

By 1785, you might have said that de Rozier was becoming over-confident. He decided to cross the English Channel by balloon. On 15 June he set off in a balloon of his own design, but disaster struck. The balloon deflated at a height of 450 metres, and plunged to the ground. De Rozier and his companion were killed – thus becoming the first air passengers to die in a crash.

The scientist who searched for the Philosopher's Stone

Isaac Newton, England (1643–1727)

There's an old story that Newton was sitting in an orchard when an apple fell to the ground, causing him to discover gravity. Sadly this is false – and there are really plenty of MUCH more bonkers things Newton ought to be famous for. How about:

Ouch!

☞ **1 Repeatedly poking himself in the eye with a needle**

Newton was interested in how light worked. He built an amazing telescope that could see into the heavens, and conducted experiments using prisms to split light. Newton was so nuts he even stuck a large needle between his eye socket and eyeball as part of an experiment. He used the needle as a way of investigating how changing the eyeball's shape affected his vision. *Don't try this at home!*

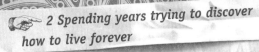

2 Spending years trying to discover how to live forever

Newton spent much of his life working on alchemy. This was an ancient, mysterious practice, which involved searching for the Philosopher's Stone. The Stone was said to turn ordinary old metal into gold.

3 Believing in loony religions

Newton almost certainly followed a religion called Arianism. Arians believed that they were special people chosen by God to rule others. This didn't go down very well with kings and queens, who thought the same thing, but about themselves.

All in all, it was a good thing that Newton got a job in charge of the Mint, where England's money was made. He gathered in all the old coins, which people had been clipping bits off for years, and made nice new ones. Anyone who was caught clipping new coins risked punishment, up to and including death.

You'd think running the Mint would have kept Newton busy – but you'd be wrong. He also found time for a HUGE argument with a German mathematician called Liebnitz (see page 64-65). Liebnitz had developed a new mathematical technique called calculus. Then Newton said HE'D actually invented calculus ages ago – he just hadn't told anyone.

When Newton died in 1727, his closest friends burnt piles of his papers (probably incriminating documents about alchemy and religion) on a bonfire. Sadly, because of the bonfire, we'll probably never know just how bonkers Newton really was.

Crackpot Quiz Question

Q. Why did it take 33 years to finish Isambard Kingdom Brunel's bridge across the Avon Gorge ...?

a) Angry mobs chasing a judge around the city made it too dangerous for work on the bridge to take place;

b) Isambard died before the bridge could be completed;

c) People were worried that the bridge was so high above the ground that it would be unsafe for humans to cross.

Mainly a), but a bit b) as well. Brunel won a competition to design the bridge in 1831, and work soon started. But then people in Bristol got really annoyed when a local judge opposed plans for them to be able to vote. They started chasing him around the city, which started a riot that carried on for three days and stopped work on the bridge. Then the money ran out. Then Isambard died, in 1859.

The bridge was finally finished, by some of Isambard's engineering buddies, in 1864.

INVENTIONS
THE WORLD TURNED OUT
NOT TO NEED

THE OIL-FIRED LIGHT BUOY

Just imagine, you're out cruising on your boat one evening when suddenly the sea turns stormy. Worse, you're accidentally pitched overboard into the choppy ocean! Thank goodness, you spot a light buoy not far away. You can just swim to that and cling to it until help comes.

The only trouble is, this is the 1800s, and the buoy you've spotted is a pre-electric, oil-fired light buoy. That's right: oil, highly flammable oil, used to power a light and all contained in a leaky buoy. Do you really want to cling to that?

On second thoughts, maybe it's better to shout really, really loud or just try and swim for land...

The mathematician who fell in love with a pigeon

Nikola Tesla, Croatia (1856–1943)

The trouble with being a genius is, sometimes people think it's too good to be true. Take Nikola Tesla, for example. At school, Nikola discovered he was really, really good at maths. In fact, he could do calculus (see pages 64-65 and 75) in his head. All of his teachers claimed he was cheating.

It's him or me, Sandra!

Next Nikola went to university. In his first year he passed all his exams with flying colours. Unfortunately, he then got addicted to gambling. By the third year – as if to prove he wasn't a *complete* genius – Nikola had lost all his living allowance, plus the money to pay his university fees. He fled to Slovenia, and only came home when the police arrested him for not having the correct papers.

Despite his slightly unusual education, Tesla got a job working in the Hungarian telephone exchange as an engineer. Then he went to France, then the USA – where he worked for Thomas Edison (see pages 32-33).

BARMY RATING: 4 OUT OF 5

He quickly fell out with Edison over money, and started up his own company, Tesla Electric Light and Manufacturing.

Tesla came up with an amazing variety of inventions during his life. The most important was the development of alternating-current electricity. This is still used to supply electricity around the world today. Edison was really annoyed, as he was trying to convince everyone his direct current was much better.

Towards the end of his life, Tesla lived in the exclusive Waldorf-Astoria hotel in New York. He'd spent most of his money on experiments, so a grateful former employer paid the bills.

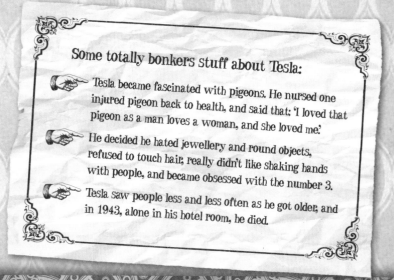

Some totally bonkers stuff about Tesla:

Tesla became fascinated with pigeons. He nursed one injured pigeon back to health, and said that: 'I loved that pigeon as a man loves a woman, and she loved me.'

He decided he hated jewellery and round objects, refused to touch hair, really didn't like shaking hands with people, and became obsessed with the number 3.

Tesla saw people less and less often as he got older, and in 1943, alone in his hotel room, he died.

ABNER DOUBLEDAY
AND BASEBALL

Who invented America's favourite game, baseball? Ask any group of people, and many of them will probably say it was Abner Doubleday, in 1839. He's said to have invented the game, thought up its name, and written down the rules in Cooperstown, New York.

The only trouble is, he didn't.

In fact, he wasn't even IN Cooperstown in 1839.

Baseball probably grew out of the traditional English game rounders. Or maybe rounders and baseball each developed at the same time from a common ancestor. Wherever it came from, though, it wasn't Abner Doubleday.

BONKERS BOFFINS

(who don't really exist)

Marisa Coulter

First off, don't call her 'Marisa'. She's Mrs Coulter to you.

You can tell Mrs Coulter's a character from a book*
rather than a real person, because she's got a daemon.
Everyone has one of these (in the books), not only
Mrs Coulter. Daemons are animals, which can
communicate with their humans. Mrs Coulter's daemon
is a nasty-tempered, vicious, golden-haired monkey.

Mrs Coulter and a bunch of bonkers boffins are involved
in a plot to separate kids from their daemons, by
cutting them away. Apparently it's for their own good
– though when someone tries to separate Mrs C. from
HER daemon, she's not all that keen.

In the end, Mrs Coulter redeems herself by dragging the
evil ruler Metatron – who's behind the whole daemon-
cutting scheme – into the Abyss, killing him and herself.

*Three books, actually: *Northern Lights* (1995), *The Subtle Knife*
(1997), and *The Amber Spyglass* (2000), by Philip Pullman.

The godfather of electronic music

Léon Theremin, Russia (1896–1993)

Léon himself was not that bonkers. His life story and the bizarre inventions he came up with, though, definitely ARE.

At the Military Engineering School one day, Léon was working on the sound system for the first-ever motion-detector burglar alarm. He noticed that the noise it made changed, depending on where he put his hand.

Léon, who loved music, quickly turned his accidental discovery into a new musical instrument. It was played by moving your hand between two antennae. You didn't have to touch it, you just moved your hand. It was called the Theremin.

The instrument wowed audiences in Russia (which had actually changed its name to the USSR, after being taken over by the communists in 1917). Then he toured Europe giving concerts. Finally, in 1927, Léon and his Theremin landed in the USA.

The USA wasn't like Russia at all. People had plenty to eat. They lived in nice apartments, drove fancy cars, and wore warm, comfortable clothes. Léon decided to stay.

Léon sold the right to make and sell Theremins to the RCA (Radio Corporation of America) company, which at first earned him quite a bit of money. The trouble was, by the 1930s the Great Depression was well under way. No one had any spare money to buy them. Léon's debts built up; to escape from them, in 1938 he went back to Russia.

The Russians were pleased to see Léon, but not in a good way. Back in 1927, they had been annoyed when one of their top boffins disappeared off to the USA. So the first thing they did was throw him in prison. They did let him out after a year or so, but only if he promised to help them make spying devices.

Léon agreed, and made:

 The Buran, which used an infrared beam to listen to conversations through a closed window.

 The Thing, a wooden replica of the Great Seal of the United States that had a bug inside. The Thing was given to the US Ambassador as a present from 'Moscow's schoolchildren', and hung inside the US Embassy for years, broadcasting secret conversations.

In the late 1980s it became possible for Russians to travel abroad again. In 1991, at the age of 95, Léon returned to the USA to give a series of Theremin concerts.

Crackpot
Quiz Question

Q. When the Danish astronomer Tycho Brahe (1546–1601) got into an argument with his cousin about mathematics, how did they sort it out ...?

a) They played paper-scissors-rock, best of three wins;

b) They put their rival equations in front of Tycho's pet elk, and asked it to decide;

c) They fought a duel. In the dark. It's the best way to settle a mathematical quarrel.

It was c), the duel. Tycho did have a pet elk, but it wasn't any good at mathematics. Happily no one died in the duel, but Tycho's nose did get cut off. For the rest of his life he wore a metal replacement, which he stuck on with glue.

INVENTIONS
THE WORLD TURNED OUT
NOT TO NEED

THE STEAM-POWERED LAWNMOVER

In Victorian times, people were mad for steam. Anything that they could, maybe, just possibly power by steam, they'd have a go. Which must be how the steam-powered lawnmower came to appear.

But this gigantic device required more of a garage than a garden shed to store it. It also took a lot longer to get started than modern lawnmowers, which you just start the engine, or plug into a socket: the huge boiler took absolutely AGES to get up a head of steam.

But perhaps the real reason the steam-powered lawnmower didn't take off is that back in the 1800s, servants were really, REALLY cheap. It was just less expensive to get your gardener to do the job.

The boffin who wrote sbɿɒwʞɔɒd

Leonardo da Vinci, Italy (1452–1519)

Like many bonkers boffins, Leonardo had a tough start in life. But he turned out to be brilliant at painting. When he was 14, he was sent to be an apprentice to a master artist called Verrocchio. A story says that one day, Leonardo was helping Verrocchio paint a picture called *The Baptism of Christ*. It is said that Verrocchio looked at the way Leonardo had painted an angel's cloak, and realised he could never paint anything that well himself. He's said to have put down his brush, and never painted again.*

Leonardo is still best known as a painter. His work includes two of the most famous paintings ever, *The Last Supper* (which took him two years to finish) and the *Mona Lisa*. But he was also good at quite a lot of other things ... including inventing.

> ✳ Sadly this story, though romantic, is almost certainly false. But it does show how good Leonardo was at painting!

Many of Leonardo's inventions could not be built in his lifetime, because the technology didn't exist. Still, his 500-year-old notebooks contain ideas for things that are familiar now, but which must have seemed **COMPLETELY** bonkers at the time.

Leonardo was fascinated with flight, and drew many pictures of birds' wings to try and understand how they worked. He designed aeroplanes, helicopters, a hang glider and a parachute. Amazingly, a hang glider based on Leonardo's design was built and successfully flown in 2002.

In his old age, Leonardo was an international celebrity. His next-door-neighbour was the King of France. As Leonardo lay dying, the King is said to have held Leonardo in his arms.

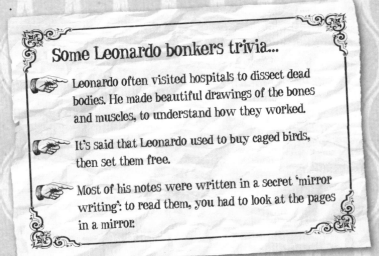

Some Leonardo bonkers trivia...

Leonardo often visited hospitals to dissect dead bodies. He made beautiful drawings of the bones and muscles, to understand how they worked.

It's said that Leonardo used to buy caged birds, then set them free.

Most of his notes were written in a secret 'mirror writing': to read them, you had to look at the pages in a mirror.

Magnificent men in flying machines

Wilbur & Orville Wright, USA (1867–1912 & 1871–1948)

Even as kids, Wilbur and Orville Wright were a bit unusual. They made stilts and started a local craze for stilt walking. They invented a machine for folding paper, and even designed a machine to take off your shoes for you. But what they REALLY wanted to do, was fly.

But there was a long way to go in the quest to build a successful airplane. People had been throwing themselves off tall buildings with feathery wings strapped to their bodies for centuries, but without much success. Lately, a few boffins had managed to glide quite a distance, but even most of these flight pioneers had eventually died when their inventions failed. To anyone who wasn't a bit bonkers, aviation wasn't really a very tempting field to go into.

On top of that, the Wrights didn't just want to glide. They wanted to be able to steer their plane, and stay in the air as long as they liked. That meant their plane needed an engine, and some sort of steering mechanism.

In the end, the Wrights had to start almost from scratch. They had to build strong wings that a) lifted the plane and b) allowed them to steer. They had to work out where the pilot should sit. They had to build an engine light enough to go on the plane (and work out where that should sit, too). They had to design propellers that would drive the plane along. Amazingly, they did it.

On 17 December 1903, Orville Wright took to the air in a plane called *Flyer*. Its first flight was a bit up-and-down, but *Flyer* took off, flew, and landed successfully. The brothers made three more flights that day, and became the first humans to take to the skies in powered flight.

Crackpot Quiz Question

Q. When the famous astronomer Nicolaus Copernicus died in 1543, was he clutching...

a) His wife and children?

b) A book?

c) A poisoned drink, given to him as a punishment for challenging the Church's views on astronomy?

It was b), a book. But not just any book: it was a book that said the Moon went round the Earth, the Earth went round the Sun, and the Sun was at the centre of the Solar System. The Church thought everything went round the Earth, so they WERE annoyed – but not annoyed enough to start poisoning people. (Nicolaus couldn't have been clutching his wife and children, as he didn't have any.)

90

INVENTIONS THE WORLD TURNED OUT NOT TO NEED

THE PEDESTRIAN CATCHER

When motorcars first appeared on the roads, pedestrians just didn't expect them to be there. They DEFINITELY didn't expect cars to be moving so fast. As a result, people kept getting run down.

The pedestrian catcher aimed to solve this problem. It was a wire-cage shovel attached to the front of the car. If a pedestrian didn't get out of the way fast enough, no problem – you just scooped them safely up! Then you could let them out when it was safe (if they'd learned their lesson)!

It *probably* goes without saying that this bonkers invention never caught on.

287-212 AD	Archimedes of Syracuse
10-70 AD	Hero of Alexandria
476 AD	**Fall of the Roman Empire**
810-887 AD	Abbas Ibn Furnas
1452-1519	Leonardo da Vinci
1492	**Columbus lands in the 'New World'**
1564-1642	Galileo Galilei
1635-1703	Robert Hooke
1643-1727	Isaac Newton
1646-1716	Gottfried Leibnitz
1692-3	**Salem witch trials**
1740-1810	Joseph-Michel Montgolfier
	(brother Jacques-Etienne 1745-99)
1775-83	**American Revolutionary War/ War of Independence**

TIMELINE

1791-1867	Michael Faraday
1800-60	Charles Goodyear
1809-92	Charles Darwin
1836-1910	Thomas Crapper
1837	**Queen Victoria becomes queen of England**
1847-1922	Alexander Graham Bell
1847-1931	Thomas Edison
1856-1943	Nikola Tesla
1867-1912	Wilbur Wright (brother Orville 1871-1948)
1867-1934	Marie Curie
1874-1937	Guglielmo Marconi
1879-1955	Albert Einstein
1881-1955	Alexander Fleming

POLITE NOTICE: entries labelled with the patented 'pointy finger' signify noteworthy historical events – thank you.

Index

TOTALLY HOOKED?

UTTERLY GRIPPED?

Then turn over
to see our other
fabulously
bonkers titles...